麦格希 中英双语阅读文库

人生品质故事集
永不放弃的梦想

【美】利姆 (Lim, A.) ●主编

张琳琳●译

麦格希中英双语阅读文库编委会●编

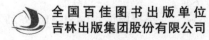

全国百佳图书出版单位
吉林出版集团股份有限公司

图书在版编目（CIP）数据

　　人生品质故事集. 永不放弃的梦想 / (美) 利姆
(Lim, A.) 主编 ; 张琳琳译 ; 麦格希中英双语阅读文库
编委会编. -- 2版. -- 长春 : 吉林出版集团股份有限
公司, 2018.3（2022.1重印）
　　（麦格希中英双语阅读文库）
　　ISBN 978-7-5581-4764-7

　　Ⅰ. ①人… Ⅱ. ①利… ②张… ③麦… Ⅲ. ①英语—
汉语—对照读物②儿童故事—作品集—世界 Ⅳ.
①H319.4：I

中国版本图书馆CIP数据核字(2018)第046444号

人生品质故事集　　永不放弃的梦想

编：	麦格希中英双语阅读文库编委会
插　画：	齐　航　李延霞
责任编辑：	朱　玲
封面设计：	冯冯翼
开　本：	660mm × 960mm　1/16
字　数：	176千字
印　张：	9.75
版　次：	2018年3月第2版
印　次：	2022年1月第2次印刷

出　版	吉林出版集团股份有限公司
发　行	吉林出版集团外语教育有限公司
地　址	长春市福祉大路5788号龙腾国际大厦B座7层
	邮编：130011
电　话	总编办：0431-81629929
	发行部：0431-81629927　0431-81629921(Fax)
印　刷	北京一鑫印务有限责任公司

ISBN 978-7-5581-4764-7　　定价：35.00元

前言 *PREFACE*

　　英国思想家培根说过：阅读使人深刻。阅读的真正目的是获取信息，开拓视野和陶冶情操。从语言学习的角度来说，学习语言若没有大量阅读就如隔靴搔痒，因为阅读中的语言是最丰富、最灵活、最具表现力、最符合生活情景的，同时读物中的情节、故事引人入胜，进而能充分调动读者的阅读兴趣，培养读者的文学修养，至此，语言的学习水到渠成。

　　"麦格希中英双语阅读文库"在世界范围内选材，涉及科普、社会文化、文学名著、传奇故事、成长励志等多个系列，充分满足英语学习者课外阅读之所需，在阅读中学习英语、提高能力。

　　◎难度适中

　　本套图书充分照顾读者的英语学习阶段和水平，从读者的阅读兴趣出发，以难易适中的英语语言为立足点，选材精心、编排合理。

◎精品荟萃

本套图书注重经典阅读与实用阅读并举。既包含国内外脍炙人口、耳熟能详的美文，又包含科普、人文、故事、励志类等多学科的精彩文章。

◎功能实用

本套图书充分体现了双语阅读的功能和优势，充分考虑到读者课外阅读的方便，超出核心词表的词汇均出现在使其意义明显的语境之中，并标注释义。

鉴于编者水平有限，凡不周之处，谬误之处，皆欢迎批评教正。

我们真心地希望本套图书承载的文化知识和英语阅读的策略对提高读者的英语著作欣赏水平和英语运用能力有所裨益。

丛书编委会

Contents

Don't Give Up Your Dream

永不放弃的梦想

Abu is one boy who never says 'Die'. The more difficult a situation is, the more he wants to do it. He just likes challenges.

situation *n.* 情况

challenge *n.* 挑战

He always says, "Challenges make life interesting."

interesting *adj.* 有趣的

He tells his friend, Ricky, he wants to make his own plane. The reply he gets from Ricky is "You're crazy." The reply does not stop him from trying to make

reply *n.* 回答；答复

阿布是一个从来不会说"放弃"的男孩。情况越困难，他就越想完成它。他就是喜欢挑战。

他总是说："挑战使生活变得有趣。"

他告诉他的朋友瑞奇，他想自己造一架飞机。他从瑞奇那儿得到的回答是："你疯了。"这样的回答没有阻止他尝试自己造飞

his own plane.

Abu loves aeroplanes. He always asks his father to take him to the airport. There, he can spend hours watching the planes. He never gets tired of seeing them fly.

He watches them land. He watches them take off. And he looks at the plane until he can see only the tail of the plane.

Then, the plane disappears. He is still

aeroplane *n.* 飞机

spend *v.* 花费

land *v.* 着陆

disappear *v.* 消失

机。

阿布喜欢飞机。他总是让父亲带他到机场。在那里，他可以花上好几个小时观察飞机，看飞机飞行，他从来不会感到厌倦。

他看着它们着陆。他看着它们起飞。他一直看着飞机，直到他的视野中只剩下飞机的尾部。

然后，飞机就消失了。可他还在盯着天空。

staring at the sky.

He always tells his parents about his ambition. His ambition is to be a pilot.

He wants to be a pilot flying his own plane.

There are many pilots. But, they do not fly their own planes.

One day, he will own a big company. The company will make planes. He will sell his planes. That is his dream.

stare *v.* 盯着看

ambition *n.* 志向

company *n.* 公司

他总是跟父母说他的志向。他的志向是做一名飞行员。

他想成为一名飞行员，驾驶自己的飞机飞翔。

有许多飞行员。但是，他们都没有驾驶自己造的飞机。

总有一天，他将拥有一家大公司。公司制造飞机。他销售自己造的飞机。这就是他的梦想。

His room is full of toy planes. His parents buy toy planes for his birthday every year. His uncles and aunts also buy only him toy planes as gifts.

There are toy planes of all designs and sizes. Some are big, some are medium and some are very small. They are of different colours. He displays the toy planes on the shelves. And he likes his visitors to look at them.

design *n.* 设计

medium *adj.*
中等的

display *v.* 展示；
陈列

shelf *n.* 架子

他的房间放满了玩具飞机。他的父母每年都买玩具飞机作为他的生日礼物。叔叔阿姨们也只给他买玩具飞机作为礼物。

玩具飞机的设计和尺寸不尽相同。有些是大型的，也有些是中型的，还有一些是小型的。它们颜色各不相同。他把玩具飞机陈列在架子上。他喜欢展示给客人们参观。

The toy planes are placed in a long row. His friends love to go to his room to see them.

    place *v.* 放置；摆放

They often say, "I like this one. No, I like that one." But, they never ask him to give them any.

They know he will never give away any of his planes. He can give them his old books or magazines but never his toy planes.

    magazine *n.* 杂志

~~~~~~

玩具飞机摆了一长排。朋友们喜欢去他的房间参观。

他们经常说："我喜欢这个。不，我喜欢那个。"但是，他们从来不问他要。

他们知道他不会赠送任何一架飞机。他能给他们旧书、旧杂志，但从来不会给他们玩具飞机。

Abu always tells them, "They are my treasure."

treasure *n.*

宝物；珍贵的东西

He tells them, "I need this collection of planes. One day, I will make my own plane."

collection *n.*

收集品；收藏品

His friends laugh when he says this. But they also know he is very serious about planes. He spends his time thinking of them. So they are not surprised. One day, Abu just might have

serious *adj.* 严肃的；

认真的

surprised *adj.* 惊奇的

阿布总是告诉他们："这些飞机是我的财富。"

他告诉他们："我需要这些飞机收集品。有一天，我还会自己制造飞机。"

每当他这么说的时候，朋友们总是笑他。但是他们也知道，他对飞机的事很认真。所以，他总是花大把的时间想飞机，朋友们也不感到惊讶。将来，也许阿布真的能拥有自己的飞机，真的能驾驶

his own plane. He will be flying his own plane!

He thinks of planes every night. His mother tells him, "In class, you do not think of planes. You think of studies. If you do not think of your studies, you will fail in all your tests."

fail *v.* 失败

He replies, "Yes, Mum. I will think of my studies. But, I think of planes at night. I dream about them. I dream of flying my

自己的飞机！

他每天晚上都思考飞机的事。母亲告诉他："上课时，你可不能想飞机的事。你得想学习上的事。如果你不想着学习，你将无法通过考试。"

他回答："知道，妈妈。我会想着学习的。但是，我在晚上会想飞机。我在梦中想着它们。我梦想着能驾驶自己造的飞机。"

own plane."

In class, he draws planes on any piece   draw v. 画
of paper he has. While waiting for class
to start, he draws pictures of planes or
makes paper planes.

His interest in planes leads to his   lead to 引起；导致
classmates and friends calling him
'Aeroplane Abu' or 'AA'.

They often say, "Mr Tan catches our
AA drawing planes instead of doing his   instead of 代替

在课堂上，阿布在他的每张纸上都画满了飞机。下课时，他也在画飞机或者折纸飞机。

他对飞机的狂热使同学和朋友都把他称作"飞机阿布"或"飞飞"。

他们常说，"谭老师发现我们的飞飞在画飞机，没有做练习

science exercises."

One night, Abu has this long dream.

In his dream, he tries to make a plane. The dream goes on for an hour.

It is a good dream to him. It starts with him busy in his workshop. First, he draws a design for his plane.

workshop *n.* 工作间

Then, he works on the wings of his plane day and night. He spends many days working on the wings. No one, not

wing *n.* 翅膀

题。"

一天晚上，阿布做了一个长长的梦。

在梦中，他尝试着造飞机。梦持续了一个小时。

对他来说，这真是个好梦。在梦中，他在工作间忙着。首先，他画了一张飞机的设计图。

然后，他不分昼夜地赶制飞机的翅膀。他花了很多天制造翅膀。一连好几个星期，没有人见到他，甚至连他的父母也没见到过

名人名言

The style is the man.

字如其人。

even his parents, sees him for weeks.

His workshop has all the tools he
needs. The pieces of metal are lying
around everywhere. The wings are on the
long table. He is working on the wings.

tool *n.* 工具

lie *v.* 平躺

He keeps on measuring them. Then,
he touches them again and again.

measure *v.* 测量

He is thinking, "These wings will make
me fly. I will be flying my first plane."

Finally, he comes out of his workshop

他。

他的工作室里到处都是他需要的工具。金属片散落一地。那对翅膀摆在长桌上。他在赶制飞机翅膀。

经过不断地检测后，他一遍又一遍地抚摸着这对翅膀。

他想，"这对翅膀将带我飞翔。我就要驾驶着我的第一架飞机飞上天了。"

最后，他微笑着走出他的工作间。这时候，他已经把自己关在

smiling. This is after shutting himself up in the workshop for a month.

He calls Ricky on the phone and says, "Tomorrow I will fly. But, I need your help."

He adds, "The wings are a bit heavy. I made them out of some scrap metal. I need you to help me drag them up to the top of the hill. With them on me I will fly."

Ricky says, "Metal! Don't you think metal is too heavy to use for wings?"

shut *v.* 关闭

scrap *n.* 碎片

drag *v.* 拽；拖

工作间里一个月了。

他给瑞奇打电话说："明天我就要飞上天了。但是，我需要你的帮助。"

他补充说："飞机的翅膀有点重。我是用废旧金属做的，所以我需要你帮我把它们拖到山顶。帮我把它们绑在身上。这样，我就可以飞了。"

瑞奇说："金属！你不认为金属太重了，不适合做翅膀吗？"

Abu says, "No, I calculated all the angles."

calculate *v.* 计算
angle *n.* 角度

Ricky just rolls his eyes. "All right. I will meet you at the hill first in the morning. We will try them out."

He is thinking, "Your wings cannot fly."

That night, Abu cannot sleep. He thinks of his 'plane' flying high.

Everyone will know about his new discovery. The reporters will flock around

flock *v.* 聚集

阿布说，"不，我计算好了所有的角度。"

瑞奇转了转眼珠说："好的。明天一早我首先就去山下见你。我们试用一下你的翅膀。"

他想："你做的翅膀飞不了的"。

那天晚上，阿布久久不能入睡。他想着他的"飞机"高高地飞在天上。

每个人都会知道他的新发现。记者会聚集在他周围采访他关于

him asking him about his machine.　　machine *n.* 机器

He will tell them about his love for planes. They will take many pictures of him and his machine with the metal wings.

The next morning, Abu and Ricky drag the wings up to the top of the hill. Ricky helps to strap the wings on for Abu.　　strap *v.*

Abu tells Ricky, "I am going to get a 用带子系（捆）好
running start. Then, I take off." He fastens　　fasten *v.* 固定

飞机的事。

　　他会告诉他们自己对飞机的热爱。他们会为他和他带有金属翅膀的飞机拍很多的照片。

　　第二天早晨，阿布和瑞奇把金属翅膀拖上了山顶。瑞奇帮着阿布把这对翅膀捆到了身上。

　　阿布告诉瑞奇："我要起跑了。然后，我就会飞起来。"他把

the pair of wings on his shoulders.

"All right. I am ready to go."

Ricky looks at the metal wings.

"Are you sure these wings are not too heavy?" he asks.

Abu says, "No, they are not. The faster I run, the lighter they will get. The wind will lift me up. I will be flying high up in the air."

He is so sure he will fly. Nobody can

shoulder *n.* 肩膀

heavy *adj.* 重的

一双翅膀固定在他肩膀上说。

"好了。我准备好了。"

瑞奇看着那对金属的翅膀。

"你确定这些翅膀不重吗?"他问。

阿布说:"不,它们不重。我跑得越快,它们就会越轻。风会将我托起。我将在高空中飞翔。"

他很肯定他会飞起来。没有人能告诉他,他戴着这对翅膀是飞

tell him he cannot fly with these wings.

So, Abu backs up about thirty feet and starts running.

But, the wings are too heavy for his legs. He gets lower and lower to the ground till he reaches the hill.

reach v. 到达

On the top of the hill, his legs become very weak. He skids across the ground and falls flat on his face.

skid v. 滑过

Ricky sees this. He rolls on the ground,

不起来的。

因此，阿布后退约三十英尺后开始跑。

可是翅膀太重了，他都走不动了。这对翅膀压在他身上，越来越重。

站在山顶时，他的腿变得没有力气了。他的腿仅仅滑了一下地面，他就脸朝下重重地摔在了地上。

瑞奇看到这个。笑翻在地，笑弯了腰。他忍不住一直笑。

名人名言

The tongue is not steel, yet it cuts.

人言可畏。

laughing his head off. He cannot stop laughing.

Ricky laughs until he and Abu get down from the hill.

That night, Abu goes back to his workshop. He shuts himself in the workshop again.

A week later, he phones Ricky again. "I did it again. I rebuilt the wings, this time, of wood and tissue paper. They are light,

rebuild v. 重做；重建
tissue n. 纸巾

直到他和阿布从山上下来，瑞奇还一直在笑。

那天晚上，阿布回到了工作室。他又把自己关在了里面。

一周后，他又打电话给瑞奇了："我又试了一次。重做了一对翅膀。这次，我用了木材和纸巾。它们很轻，所以我可以从屋顶上

so I can jump off the roof."

Ricky is to meet him on top of the roof this time. He sighs. He knows what to expect this time.

sigh *v.* 叹气

The next morning, Ricky goes to the top of the roof. Abu is ready to take off. He has on a pair of strange-looking wings. They are paper wings.

ready *adj.* 准备好的

Ricky is surprised. He asks, "So, you think you are going to jump off and fly

surprised *adj.* 惊讶的

起飞。"

瑞奇这次要去屋顶找他了。他叹了一口气。他预料到会发生什么。

隔天早上，瑞奇去了屋顶。阿布做好了起飞的准备。他有一双看起来奇怪的翅膀。它们是纸做的翅膀。

瑞奇很惊讶。他问："你真的想跳下来，戴着这对翅膀飞翔

with these wings?"

Abu is too busy fixing the wings to answer. He also thinks there is no need to answer Ricky.

fix *v.* 使固定；安装

Abu backs up a little and jumps. SMACK! SMACK!

back *v.* 后退

The wings break immediately. He lands on his head in the middle of some bushes.

Luckily, he is not hurt. He is lying in

hurt *adj.* 受伤的

吗？"

    阿布忙着固定翅膀，没有回答。他也认为没有必要回答瑞奇。

    阿布向后退了退，然后跳了下去。啪！啪！

    翅膀立即断裂了。他摔倒在灌木丛中。

    幸运的是，他没有受伤。他躺在了灌木丛中。

the bushes.

Again, Ricky rolls around on the ground laughing for a minute. He gets up and asks Abu if he is all right.

"Yes, Yes," says Abu. "I guess the wings are a little weak. I know the shape is just right. I will go back to the workshop."

"I will make another pair of wings out of another material. Something is not as

guess *v.* 猜想

weak *adj.* 脆弱的

material *n.* 材料

~~~~~~

瑞奇再次笑翻在地。他起身问阿布怎么样。

"挺好，没事，"阿布回答，"我想这对翅膀有点脆弱。我知道它的形状是正确的。我要回到工作室去。"

"我会用其他的材料再重新做一对翅膀。一种没有旧金属重也

heavy as the scrap metal and not as light as the tissue paper."

He adds, "I know what to do about the wings this time."

Ricky cannot believe what he hears.   hear *v.* 听见
Abu is going to try again!

Abu goes back to his workshop. This time, he stays there for two weeks.

Working hard, he makes another pair   hard *adv.* 努力地
of wings. They are not made of paper or

不像纸巾那么轻的材料。"

他补充说："这次，我知道该怎么做翅膀了。"

瑞奇不敢相信自己的耳朵。阿布还要再次尝试！

阿布回到了工作室。这一次，他在那儿待了两周。

经过了艰苦地工作，他又做了一对翅膀。它们不是用纸或金属

metal.

This time, he will fly. Ricky is very sure of that. He must not fail again.

A month later, he calls Ricky. Of course, he says the same thing.

This time, Ricky knows what to expect. He is thinking, "Another good laugh. I just hope it will not take too long. I have many things to do."

He is thinking Abu wastes too much

expect *v.* 期待

waste *v.* 浪费

做的。

这次，他会飞起来的。阿布对此很清楚。他不会再失败了。

一个月后，他打电话给瑞奇。当然，他说的还是那件事情。

这一次，瑞奇能预料出结果。他想："又是另外一个笑话。我只是希望时间不会太长。我还有好多事要做。"

他觉得阿布在他的飞机上浪费了太多的时间。不过无论如何，

time on his planes. Anyway, he agrees to help Abu.

Ricky arrives at his house the next day. He looks at the wings. They look good! No more metal or paper. Abu spends a lot of time improving them.

arrive *v.* 到达

improve *v.* 改善；提高

Abu says, "This time, I made them out of wax and wood. There is a handle under each wing for me to move the wing up and down. I can fly this time."

wax *n.* 蜡

他还是同意帮阿布的忙。

第二天，瑞奇来到了他家。他看到了那对翅膀。它们看起来不错！不是用金属做的，也不是用纸做的。阿布花了很多时间，改善它们的性能。

阿布说："这次，我是用蜡和木头制作的这对翅膀。在每只翅膀下面有一个手柄，我可以用它来操控翅膀。这次，我一定能飞起来。"

"I need you to help me strap them on," says Abu.

Ricky helps him to strap the wings on. They fit very well.

fit *v.* 合适

There is a belt around his waist. This is to make sure he will not fall off when flying. He looks ready to fly. He also looks confident.

belt *n.* 带子

"Here we go!" Abu yells. He backs up and begins running towards the top of

yell *v.* 大喊；大叫

"我需要你帮我把它们绑在身上。"阿布说。

瑞奇帮他戴上翅膀。它们很合适。

在他的腰间有一条带子，这是为了确保他不会在飞行中掉下来。他看起来已经做好了飞行的准备。他也很有信心。

"出发吧！"阿布大叫。他后退一下，开始朝山顶跑。在小山

the hill. At the edge of the hill, he starts
to lift up into the air.

    He is flying! He is really flying. He flies
higher and higher. It is a great feeling to
fly.

    "YAHOOO!" he yells again. He is really
getting high now.

    He is flying above his house. He is
flying above his neighbour's house and
many other houses. The feeling is great.

edge *n.* 边缘

neighbour *n.* 邻居

的边缘，他开始跃起，飞到了空中。

    他在飞！他真的在飞，他飞得越来越高，飞翔是一种很棒的感
觉。

    "呀呼！"他大声喊道。他真的是越飞越高了。

    他飞到了他家的上空，他邻居家的上空，许多别人家的上空。
他感觉很棒。

Then, he starts to worry. "How do I land?" he asks himself. He also notices his wings are starting to melt.

worry *v.* 担心

melt *v.* 融化

He is rising so high. The sun is melting the wax on the wings.

Soon, he has tiny wings. And he is going to crash into the trees!

crash *v.* 撞

"Oh! Oh! This is going to hurt," says Abu to himself.

He crashes into the trees.

随后，他开始担心。"我该如何着陆呢？"他问自己。他也注意到了他的翅膀正在融化。

他飞得太高了。太阳把翅膀上的蜡烤化了。

很快，他的翅膀变小了。他要撞到树上了！

"哦！哦！这次我要受伤了。"他自言自语道。

他从天上掉了下来，撞到了树上。

BANG!

Ricky runs to him and asks, "Are you all right?"

Abu answers, "I think so. Well, I flew just now. I made my own plane."

He is hurt with a few cuts, but he is feeling too happy to feel the pain.

pain *n.* 疼痛

His mother comes to wake him up to get ready for school. Abu is still smiling.

wake *v.* 叫醒

She asks, "Why are you smiling early in

嘭！

瑞奇跑过来问："你还好吗？"

阿布回答："我想还好。我刚才飞起来了。我自己制造了飞机。"

他受了几处割伤。但是他太高兴了，以至于感觉不到疼痛。

妈妈叫他起床，准备去学校。阿布嘴角依然挂着微笑。

她问："你为什么一大早就这么高兴？发生什么好事了？"

the morning? Something nice happening today?"

happen *v.* 发生

He tells her, "I had the best dream. In my dream, I made my plane. I flew it in the sky."

His mother is thinking, "He has his madness about his planes. Even in sleep, he thinks of them."

madness *n.* 疯狂

And so Abu invents his own plane in his dream. The dream keeps him happy and smiling for a long time.

～～～～～～～～～～～～～～～～～～～～～～

他告诉妈妈："我做了一个很棒的梦。在梦里，我坐着自己的飞机，飞上了天空。"

他妈妈想："他对飞机太痴迷了。即便在睡梦中，他也在想着飞机。"

就这样，阿布在睡梦中发明了自己的飞机。这个梦使他很开心，他笑了好久。

Lost in the Jungle

在丛林中迷路了

The place Dolah lives in is next to the jungle. It is a farm. He lives on the farm with his family.

jungle *n.* 丛林

The farm is just outside of the jungle. It is called a jungle farm.

There are about twenty such jungle farms. The farmers live on the jungle farms with their families. They grow crops on their farms. Sometimes, they go to the jungle to collect firewood.

firewood *n.* 木柴

多拉住的地方在丛林边上。那是一块农场。他与家人一起生活在农场。

农场就在丛林外面。这样的农场被称为丛林农场。

这附近大约有二十个丛林农场。农民们与家人在丛林农场中一起生活。他们在农场种庄稼。有时，他们也会去丛林拾柴火。

The people live simple lives. All of them are farmers. They are poor but happy. The familes are close to each other.

They grow vegetables and fruit trees. They also keep chickens and goats. Sometimes, the chickens and goats stray away from the farm.

They go into the jungle to look for their chickens and goats.

Dolah fears the jungle. He is not like all

simple *adj.* 简单的

stray *v.* 迷路；走失

人们过着简单的生活。他们都是农民。虽然贫穷但很快乐。家人间也亲密无间。

他们种植蔬菜和果树。他们还饲养鸡和山羊。有时，鸡和山羊会从农场走失。

他们就会去丛林中寻找他们的鸡和山羊。

多拉不敢去丛林。他跟其他男孩不太一样，他很容易受到惊

the other boys. He gets frightened easily.

The other boys like to tease him. They call him 'coward'.

The boys like to go into the jungle during the day. It is so quiet. All they can hear are the insects and leaves.

They step on the leaves on the jungle floor. The leaves make some kind of nice noise.

So, Dolah stays away from the jungle

frightened *adj.* 害怕的

tease *v.* 嘲笑；戏弄

coward *n.* 懦夫；
        胆小鬼

insect *n.* 昆虫

吓。

其他的男孩都喜欢捉弄他。他们叫他 "胆小鬼"。

孩子们在白天的时候喜欢去丛林。这个时候的丛林很安静。他们只能听到昆虫的鸣叫和树叶的沙沙声。

他们踩踏着丛林地上的落叶，树叶发出美妙的声响。

而多拉却总是尽可能地远离丛林。他听说许多关于丛林中野兽

as much as possible. He hears many stories about the wild animals in the jungle. The stories scare him.

wild *adj.* 野性的

scare *v.* 使……害怕

Sometimes, he has nightmares thinking of the stories he hears.

nightmare *n.* 噩梦

He also hears of animals killing people for their food. These people go into the jungle. But, they do not come out.

The villagers talk among themselves.

villager *n.* 村民

"Ah Hock went to the jungle yesterday.

的故事，这些故事把他吓坏了。

有时，他一想到这些故事，就会做噩梦。

他还听说这些野兽会吃人。有些人走进丛林就再也没出来。

这些故事在村民中流传。

"阿福昨天去了丛林，他迷路了。他的家人正在等他回家，他

He got lost in it. His family is waiting for him to come home. They think the animals killed him."

Another farmer said, "They ate his body and left the head on the ground."

Hearing these stories, Dolah will run as far as he can away from the jungle.

In Dolah's mind, the jungle is a bad place. People enter it and never come out alive. Their bodies rot on the ground.

enter v. 进入

rot v. 腐烂

们猜测他被野兽吃了。"

另一个农民说："他的身体被野兽吃光了，只剩下了头。"

听到这些故事，多拉就会尽可能远地跑离丛林。

在多拉心里，丛林是一个糟糕的地方。人们只要走进去就不会活着出来。他们的尸体会烂在地上。

He does not believe the other boys. They tell him the jungle is exciting. It offers many adventures beyond their dreams.

believe *v.* 相信

exciting *adj.*
令人兴奋的

adventure *n.* 冒险

His mind is made up. No going into jungle for him!

That evening, Dolah got lost in the jungle. His father, Ali, sent him to look for two of their chickens.

They did not return to their coop.

coop *n.* 笼子

他不相信那些男孩子们。他们对他说丛林令人神往，他们在丛林中经历过许多意想不到的冒险历程。

他主意已定。绝对不去丛林！

可是一天晚上，多拉却在丛林里迷路了。他的父亲阿里，派他去寻找家里的两只鸡。

这两只鸡没回笼子。

名人名言

The water that bears the boat is the same that swallows it up.

水能載舟，亦能覆舟。

Usually before dark, Ali calls out to his chickens and goats. On hearing his call, they will come running back to their coop. And they stay there till the next morning.

But, that evening, they did not come back. Dolah's elder brother went to town.

elder *adj.* 年长的

He would not be back till late in the evening.

So, Ali sent Dolah to go and look for

通常在天黑之前，阿里呼喊他的鸡和山羊。听到他的呼喊，它们会回到它们的笼子，一直呆到第二天早上。

但是，那天晚上，那两只鸡没有回来。多拉的哥哥去了镇上，要很晚才能回来。

所以，阿里就派多拉去找鸡。

the chickens.

Ali warned him, "You have to come with the chickens back before it is dark. Come back before the evening prayers."

Dolah searched everywhere. But he could not find the two chickens. He searched under the house. He searched the back of the garden. He searched under the trees.

They were not around. So, he found

warn	v. 警告；提醒
prayer	n. 祈祷
search	v. 搜寻

阿里警告他："你在天黑前要把鸡带回来。一定要赶在晚上祷告之前回来。"

多拉到处寻找，也没找到那两只鸡。他去了房檐底下，花园后面，大树底下。

哪儿都没有。不知不觉中，他发现自己来到了丛林。他想转身

himself walking towards the jungle. He wanted to turn back.

But he remembered his father's words, "Come back with the chickens."

For once, he would make his father proud of him. He would come back with the two chickens.

He was thinking, "I will not come back without the chickens."

So, he continued walking to the jungle.

towards *prep.* 朝向

proud *adj.* 骄傲的；
自豪的

continue *v.* 继续

回去。

但他想起了父亲的话："把鸡带回来。"

这次，他要让父亲为他骄傲。他会把两只鸡带回来。

他想："找不到鸡，我绝不回去。"

于是，他硬着头皮继续往丛林走。

And he entered it trying to feel brave.

He walked and walked. Soon, he wandered too deep into the jungle. He kept on shouting, "Cluck! Cluck! Cluck!"

But, no chickens ran to him. He was too far inside the jungle.

He looked around him. He looked at the trees. He did not know where he was! He could not tell which way he came from.

brave *adj.* 勇敢的

wander *v.* 闲逛

cluck *n.*

（鸡的）咕咕声

他鼓起勇气走进了丛林。

他走着走着，很快就走到了丛林深处。他不停地喊："咕咕！咕咕！咕咕！"

但是，根本就没有鸡跑过来。他走出太远了。

他环顾四周，打量着周围的树。他分辨不出方向了！他找不到来时的路了。

It was clear that Dolah was lost in the jungle. It was getting dark. He did not bring along any torch.

torch *n.* 火把

What was he to do? He was starting to feel afraid. He was afraid of the dark. He was afraid of the wild animals.

At the same time, he was still thinking of the chickens. "Where are the two chickens? I must find them."

So, he shouted, "Cluck! Cluck!"

shout *v.* 叫喊

显然，多拉在丛林中迷路了。天色渐渐暗了下来。可是他没带火把。

怎么办呢？他开始感到害怕了。他害怕黑暗，害怕野兽。

即使在这个时候，他仍然在想："那两只鸡在哪儿？我必须找到它们。"

他又喊着："咕咕！咕咕！"

He was asking himself, "How am I going to find my way back?"

Then, he heard the evening prayers from the village mosque. It was getting late. Soon, it would be completely dark.

His father said, "Come back before the evening prayers."

Oh dear! And he did not know where he was. He did not know how to get out of the jungle.

mosque *n.* 清真寺

completely *adv.* 完全地

他心里想："我怎么才能找到回去的路呢？"

不一会儿，他听到村里清真寺传出了晚祷声。天黑了下来。很快，就完全的黑了。

父亲跟他说过："一定要在晚祷前回来。"

怎么办呀！他不知道自己在哪儿，也不知道怎么才能走出丛林。

名人名言

The wise man knows he knows nothing, the fool thinks he knows all.

清者自清，浊者自浊。

He could not hear the prayers any more. Everywhere was silent.

silent *adj.* 安静的

Of course, he could hear the leaves crackling under his feet.

crackle *v.* 发出噼啪声

He was in the jungle for about two hours. He thought he heard a wild animal.

Was it a tiger? Was it a wild boar? He did not want to think of that at all. He was too afraid to think of that.

boar *n.* 野猪

他听不到祷告声了，周围一片寂静。

他只能听到树叶在脚下噼啪作响。

他已经在丛林中待了两个多小时了。他好像听到了野兽的声音。

是老虎吗？还是野猪？他不愿去想，也不敢想。

Then, he started running wildly like a mad person. He kept on falling to the jungle floor.

mad *adj.* 疯的

He picked himself up and ran again. And he would fall again. He was crying out loudly now. He was covering his face. He was pulling his hair!

cover *v.* 覆盖

pull *v.* 拉

He was even thinking, "This is the end of me. A wild animal is coming to eat me."

然后，他开始像疯了一样疯狂地奔跑。他不断地在丛林中跌倒。

然后，他又爬起来接着跑。他还会再次跌倒。他大声叫喊着，捂着脸，揪自己的头发！

他甚至在想的："我要死了。野兽来吃我了。"

He told his wife, "I should not ask him to go and look for the chickens. He is a timid boy. He is scared of the dark."

timid *adj.* 胆小的

His wife was angry with him. "Why did you ask him then?"

Then, she started crying, "If anything happens to him..."

Ali stopped her and said, "Nothing will happen to him. We have to go and look for him."

look for 寻找

阿里对妻子说："我真不应该让他去找鸡。他胆子太小，怕黑。"

妻子很生他的气："那你为什么还要让他去呢？"

接着，她哭了起来："要是他发生意外……"

阿里打断她说："他不会有事的。我们得去找他。"

The family started dinner without Dolah. Both father and mother just stared at the food on the table.

stare *v.* 盯着看

They could not eat without knowing where Dolah was.

Where was he? He should be back with the chickens.

They knew he had lost his way. Could he not find his way back?

It did not cross their minds Dolah

cross...mind
掠过心头

吃晚餐了，多拉还没回来。他的父母只是盯着桌上的食物。

没找到多拉，他们吃不下。

他在哪儿？他应该带着鸡回来了。

他们知道多拉可能迷路了。难道他找不到回来的路了？

他们根本没想到多拉会走进丛林。

would enter the jungle.

His father told his mother, "Dolah will
never go into the jungle. It frightens him." frighten *v.* 使害怕

His mother said angrily, "You asked
him to look for the chickens. He walked
into the jungle to look for them. He
wanted to come back with the chickens."

At ten o'clock, ALi walked to the the Village Headman
Village Headman's house. 村长

He had to ask for help. He was sure

父亲对母亲说："多拉不会去丛林。他不敢。"

母亲生气地说："你让他找鸡。他一定到丛林中去找了。他想
把鸡找回来。"

晚上十点，阿里来到村长家。

他来求助。他确信多拉在丛林中迷路了。

Dolah was lost in the jungle.

He could not go into the jungle alone at night.

alone *adv.* 单独

"Tuan, my son is in the jungle. I think he is lost in the jungle. I need people to go with me to look for him."

need *v.* 需要

On hearing that, the Village Headman quickly called a search party. There were four men, Ali, the Headman and two of their friends.

他不能独自一人在晚上去丛林。

"老段，我的儿子在丛林中。我想他一定是在丛林中迷路了。我需要有人和我一起去找他。"

听到这话，村长赶紧叫人来帮忙寻找。阿里、村长还有他们的两个朋友组成了四个人的搜寻队。

They were also farmers whose farms were nearby. They were willing to help one of their villagers in trouble. Carrying strong torches, they walked into the jungle to look for Dolah.

trouble *n.* 困难；麻烦

Back in the jungle, poor Dolah was sitting on the jungle floor. He was tired after all the running.

poor *adj.* 可怜的

He had to keep slapping his arms and legs.

slap *v.* 拍打

他们都是附近农场的农民。他们愿意帮助遇到困难的村民。于是，他们带着火把，去丛林寻找多拉。

丛林中，可怜的多拉坐在地上。跑了这么久，他累了。

他不停地拍打着胳膊和腿。

There were many mosquitoes biting him. He had to keep the mosquitoes away.

mosquito *n.* 蚊子

He was not only tired. He was thirsty, hungry and frightened.

He stood up and looked at the trees. He tried to look for some signs to help him recognize where he was.

sign *n.* 标记

recognize *v.* 辨认

But, he did not see any. He walked for another twenty minutes.

有好多蚊子咬他。他得不断地驱赶蚊子。

除了累，他还又渴又饿又害怕。

他站起来看着树，他试图找到一些标记帮他辨别方向。

但是，他什么也没找到。他又走了二十分钟。

He was really tired. All seemed lost.

What should he do? Would he ever get out alive?

He could not walk any more. So, he was lying on the jungle floor, half crying and half praying. He was starting to feel sleepy.

sleepy *adj.* 困倦的

His body, arms and legs were aching very badly. The mosquitoes kept on biting his face, hands and legs.

ache *v.* 疼痛

他真的很累了。完全找不到方向。

他该怎么办？他能活着走出去吗？

他再也走不动了。于是，他躺在地上，一边哭一边祈祷。不知不觉地，他有点困了。

他的身体、手臂和腿疼得要命。蚊子一直在叮他的脸、胳膊和腿。

He had cuts and mosquito bites all over his arms and legs.

Yet, he could do nothing. It was completely dark.

He was alone. He did not know he would still be alive in the morning.

He tried to close his eyes and imagined he was at home with his family. His mother would be putting his plate of rice before him. They would talk while they

imagine *v.* 想象

plate *n.* 一盘

胳膊和腿上都是伤和蚊子叮咬的包。

而他却什么也做不了。天太黑了。

他独自一人。他不知道天能否活到明天早晨。

他试着闭上眼睛，想象着他和家人待在家里。母亲把一盘米饭放在他面前。他们一边吃饭一边聊天。

ate.

The search party shone their torches. They were walking into the jungle.

Ah Hock said, "Ali, are you sure your son is here?"

Another farmer, Ahmad, said, "He would be very frightened. Even a brave man would be scared to be in the jungle at this time."

The two men looked at the darkness.

darkness *n.* 黑暗

搜寻队点亮了火把，走进丛林。

阿福说："阿里，你确定你儿子在这儿吗？"

另一个农民艾哈迈德说："他肯定吓坏了。即使一个勇敢的成年人夜晚在丛林中也会害怕。"

他们俩看着黑暗的丛林。

Ali heard this. He felt very sad.

He was till thinking, "Why did I ask him to look for the chickens?" He would not go home without his son.

It could take the whole night. It could take many more days. He must bring back his son with him. His wife must see their son again.

whole *adj.* 完整的

He started praying silently.

silently *adv.* 默默地

"Please let Dolah be all right." At that

阿里听到这儿，感到很悲伤。

他在想："我为什么要让他去找鸡？"找不到儿子，他决不回家。

就算找上一整晚，找上好多天。他也要把儿子找回来。一定要让妻子见到儿子。

他开始默默地祈祷。

"请保佑多拉。"那一刻，他的祈祷起作用了。

名人名言

The wolf has a winning game when the shepherds quarrel.

螳螂捕蝉，黄雀在后。

moment, his prayer was answered.

At that minute, Dolah thought he heard the clucking of chickens. He got up and limped all the way. He was following the sound. The sound got louder and louder.

limp *v.* 瘸着走

The sound was leading him out of the jungle.

lead *v.* 引导；带领

Dolah walked faster and faster. Then, he heard his father's voice. He cried out, "Father! Father!"

与此同时，多拉似乎听到了鸡叫。他站起来，顺着声音的方向，一瘸一拐地往前走。声音越来越大了。

声音带着他走出了丛林。

多拉越走越快。然后，他听到了父亲的声音。他大声喊："爸爸！爸爸！"

The search party heard him. They saw him running to them.

Dolah saw their torches. ALi ran forward and hugged his son. Together, they walked back to their house.

hug *v.* 拥抱

Soon, they could see the fire burning at the back of their house.

burn *v.* 燃烧

The story went round about Dolah.

He was not a timid boy any more. He was lost in the jungle for a few hours at

timid *adj.* 胆小的

搜寻队听到了他的喊声，看到他向他们跑过来。

多拉看见火把。阿里跑向儿子，把他紧紧地抱在怀里。

他们一起往家走。

很快，他们就看到了房子后院的炉火。

多拉的故事很快就传开了。

他不再是那个胆小的男孩了。他在夜晚的丛林里迷失了几个小

night.

"What a brave boy!" Everyone seemed to be saying.

As for Dolah, he was thinking, "Maybe, I am not that frightened of the jungle after all. It is not such a frightening place."

frightening *adj.*
使人恐惧的

~~~~~~

时。

"真是一个勇敢的男孩！"每个人似乎都在说。

至于多拉，他想："也许，我并不那么害怕丛林。也许它也没有那么可怕。

Mother's Love

母亲的爱

生日快乐

往年一张粗糙的生日卡片

诠释了母爱

Maria was a widow. Her husband passed away seven years ago. Her son, Sam, was only two years old. Sam could not remember much of his father.

widow *n.* 寡妇

She had to raise Sam alone. Her husband died without leaving any money.

raise *v.* 抚养

She had to work to feed her son. She worked hard as a tailor, hawker and maid day and night.

hawker *n.* 小贩

Maria and her son lived in a wooden

玛利亚是个寡妇。七年前她的丈夫去世的时候，儿子山姆只有两岁。山姆对父亲的印象很模糊。

她独自一人抚养山姆。丈夫去世时，什么都没有留下。

她不得不出去工作，养活儿子。她没白天没黑夜地努力工作，做着裁缝，小贩和女仆。

玛利亚和她的儿子住在一个小木屋里。房子虽然很旧，但是仍

house. It was old. But, it was still a house. There was one bedroom and a kitchen at the back.

It was in this house that Sam grew up. It was here Maria held Sam and told him bedtime stories.

grow up 长大

It was here she looked after him. He had chicken pox. She stayed up the whole night looking after him.

chicken pox 水痘

Sam was a good child. He always

然能为他们遮风挡雨。这所房子只有一间卧室，卧室后面是厨房。

就是在这个房子里，山姆长大了。就是在这里，玛利亚抱着山姆给他讲睡前故事。

就是在这里，她照顾他。他得水痘的时候，她照顾了他一整夜。

山姆是个好孩子。他总是听母亲的话。他用斧头砍柴，放进厨

obeyed his mother. He cut firewood with an axe. He carried it to their stove in the kitchen. Then, he made a fire with it.

He walked to the main taps along the road. Then, he carried pails of water back to the house.

In the kitchen, he waited for his mother to cook him dinner.

Mother and son were very close. They had only each other.

obey *v.* 遵从

stove *n.* 炉子

pail *n.* 一桶（的量）

房的炉子里。然后，他用这些木柴生火。

他沿着小路去公用水龙头接水。然后，他把水抬回家。

他在厨房，等妈妈给他做晚餐。

母子俩相依为命。

Sam learnt manners from his mother. He learnt to be hardworking like his mother.

He studied hard in school to please her. He got good grades to make her happy.

Sam wanted to be rich one day. He wanted to live happily with his mother.

The years passed fast. Sam sat for his examination. He passed with good

manner *n.* 礼貌

hardworking *adj.* 努力工作的

please *v.* 使……开心

examination *n.* 考试

～～～～～～～～～～～～～～～～～～～～～～

　　山姆从母亲那儿学会了彬彬有礼，学会了像母亲一样吃苦耐劳。

　　他在学校努力学习，使母亲开心。取得好成绩，使她快乐。

　　山姆梦想有一天能变得富有，他想跟妈妈在一起幸福快乐地生活。

　　日子过得很快。一转眼，山姆小学毕业了。他以优异的成绩通

grades.

His mother was very happy. She told her friends, "My Sam will become a lawyer one day."

"Then, we can get out from this village. I am waiting only for that day."

Sam went to secondary school. He continued to get good grades in his examinations.

lawyer *n.* 律师

secondary *adj.*
中等教育的

过了考试。

　　玛利亚很高兴。她对朋友说："我的山姆会成为一名律师。"

　　"然后，我们就可以离开这个村子了。我一直等着这一天。"

　　山姆上了中学。他仍然成绩优异。

Then, he went to a college in England.

She had to work harder. She sewed clothes till midnight. She sewed the clothes on an old sewing machine. She made cakes to sell at a roadside stall. With the money, she sent him to college.

She used to tell him, "Son, I have to send you to college. I don't care if I work twenty hours a day. You must go to college. You must have a good job when

college *n.* 大学

sew *v.* 缝

stall *n.* 小摊

然后，他去了英国读大学。

玛利亚工作得更努力了。她通宵达旦地缝衣服。她用一台旧缝纫机缝衣服。她把做好的蛋糕放在路边的小摊上出售。她用赚到的钱供山姆读大学。

她告诉过山姆："儿子，我得供你上大学。我不在乎一天工作二十小时。你必须读大学。长大后，你必须找到好工作。"

名人名言

The world is a ladder for some to go up and others to go down.

世界如阶梯，有人上有人下。

you grow up."

He listened to these words. And he answered, "I will look after you, Mummy. You will grow old with me around."

She would kiss him. His words made her very happy.

She only waited for him to grow up. Then, she could stop working.

He would look after her. It was his turn

wait *v.* 等待

stop *v.* 停止

turn *n.*

（依次轮到的）机会

听了这些话，山姆说："我会照顾你的，妈妈。我会给你养老。"

这时，她会吻他。他的话使她很高兴。

她只等着他长大。然后，她就不用工作了。

他会照顾她。轮到他照顾她了。没有什么比跟儿子在一起生活

to care for her. Nothing would make her as happy as living with her son. He would have a good job. They would move to live in the city.

He spent three years in a college in England. He was studying to get a degree. The fees were high. She had to send him more money. She even had to go on her bicycle collecting old newspaper to sell.

spend *v.* 花费

fee *n.* 费用

collect *v.* 收集

更让她高兴的事儿了。他会找到好工作。他们会搬到城里住。

他在英国读三年大学，然后会获得学位。学费很高，她不得不给他寄更多的钱。她甚至骑着旧自行车收旧报纸卖。

She was doing four jobs. She was a tailor at night, an office cleaner in the morning, a hawker in the afternoon and a newspaper collector in the evening.

cleaner *n.* 清洁工

collector *n.* 收集者

It was a hard life for her. The neighbours all knew her. It was common to see her riding her old bicycle.

common *adj.* 普遍的

She went from house to house to collect old newspapers. Many knew she was coming on her bicycle. They kept

她同时做四份工作。夜里做缝纫活。早晨打扫卫生。下午卖东西。晚上收报纸。

她过着艰辛的生活。邻居们都认识她。总是看到她骑在自行车上。

她一家一户地收集旧报纸。许多人知道她会骑着自行车来收报

their newspapers for her.

They would say, "These are for poor Maria."

She was cycling on her bicycle. They said, "Here comes Maria. Give her the newspapers."

They all knew she worked hard to support her son in college.

And they said, "Hope Sam will be kind to her. Hope he knows his mother's love

cycle *v.* 骑自行车

support *v.* 支持；
供养

纸，他们会把报纸给她留着。

他们会说："这是给可怜的玛利亚的。"

她骑着自行车过来时，他们说："玛利亚来了。把报纸给她。"

他们都知道她努力工作供儿子读大学。

他们说："希望山姆能善待她。希望他了解母亲对他的爱。"

for him."

They were not so sure he would do that.

The years passed. Sam was busy with his studies. During those three years, he came back only once. His reason was 'I'm busy with my classes and tests."

reason *n.* 理由

That time he came back was the Chinese New Year. Even that, he stayed for only one day.

~~~~~~~~~~~~~~~~~~~~~~~~~~~~~~~~~~~~

他们不太确定他会孝敬母亲。

日子一天天过去。山姆忙着学习。在这三年中，他只回来过一次。他的理由是："我在忙着学习和考试。"

那次他回来的时候是农历新年。即使在这样的节日，他也只在家待了一天。

He said he had to rush back to the college. He had revision to do.

revision *n.* 修改

One day, Maria was very sick. Her neighbour, Mrs Choo, came to see her. Mrs Choo boiled medicine for her.

boil *v.* 煮；熬

She told Mrs Choo not to tell Sam. She did not want him to come home. He was too busy with his studies.

Mrs Choo felt sorry for Maria. She did

他说他要赶回学校，修改论文。

有一天，玛利亚得了重病。她的邻居周太太来看望她，给她熬了药。

她告诉周太太不要告诉山姆，她不想让他回家。他正忙于学习。

周太太觉得玛利亚很可怜，她认为她儿子没有忙着学习。

名人名言

The world is but a little place, after all.

海内存知己，天涯若比邻。

not think her son was that busy with his studies.

Mrs Choo went to Maria's house every day for a week. She boiled her medicine. She cooked her porridge.

porridge *n.* 粥

Slowly, Maria got better. Yet, Sam did not know anything about this.

Maria phoned him to tell him she was well and strong. He was not to worry about her.

well *adj.* 健康的

周太太连着一星期每天都来看望玛利亚。给她熬药，为她做粥。

玛利亚一点点地好了起来。山姆根本就不知道这件事。

玛利亚给他打电话，告诉他她很健康，不用担心她。

On the phone, he told her not to phone him so often. He was too busy to talk to her.

After her illness, she was getting weak. Her legs were always painful.

illness *n.* 病

painful *adj.* 疼痛的

Her eyes were tired. She did not have enough sleep.

Her sister, Lily, came to live with her for a month. Lily had a daughter, Kate.

在电话里，他告诉她不要总给他打电话。他太忙了，没时间和她聊天。

这场病过后，她身体越来越坏了。她的腿老疼。

她的眼睛累坏了，她睡眠不足。

她的妹妹，莉莉，来跟她住了一个月。她有一个女儿，叫凯

Kate stayed back to help her aunt to do housework.

She felt pity for her sickly and weak aunt.

Kate went to a nearby school. She helped her aunt do the washing and cooking.

Maria was too weak to do heavy housework. She no longer stayed up to do sewing. Luckily, she saved enough for

sickly *adj.* 常生病的

weak *adj.* 虚弱的

特。她把凯特留下来，帮玛利亚做家务。

凯特同情她体弱多病的姨妈。

凯特转到了附近的一个学校读书。她帮姨妈洗衣做饭。

玛利亚太虚弱了，做不了繁重的家务。她不能再熬夜做缝纫活

her meals and Sam's college fees.

Kate mopped the floor. She cleaned   mop v. 用拖把擦干净
the windows.

At night, Maria and Kate took dinner
together. They always talked about Sam.

Maria thought of Sam all the time. Her
tired eyes brightened. She could spend   brighten v. 发亮
hours telling Kate about Sam as a boy.

It went on and on. "Sam did this, Sam
did that. Sam liked to eat this. Sam said

了。所幸，她存够了自己的生活费和山姆的大学学费。

凯特帮姨妈拖地板，擦窗户。

到了晚上，玛利亚和凯特一起吃晚餐。她们总是谈论山姆。

玛利亚一直惦念着山姆。她疲惫的眼睛放着光芒，她可以花上好几个小时给凯特讲山姆小时候的事。

她不停地讲着："山姆做了这个，山姆做了那个，山姆喜欢吃

this."

Kate listened to Maria talk about Sam. She was thinking, "Hope Sam will not forget about his mother's love for him."

forget v. 忘记

Maria spent long hours staring at the old photographs of Sam. There was one of Sam going to school on his first day. There was Sam at his school party. This one showed Sam winning medals on

photograph n. 照片

medal n. 奖牌

这个，山姆说过这样的话。"

凯特听玛利亚谈论山姆。她想，"希望山姆不会忘记母亲对他的爱。"

玛利亚盯着山姆以前的照片一看就是好几个小时。有山姆第一天上学的，有山姆参加学校派对的，还有山姆在运动会上夺得奖牌的。

Sports Day.

Maria could not wait for him to come back.

She would go and live with him in the city. Surely, he would find a job in the city.

surely *adv.* 想必

One day, Mrs Choo came to tell her. There was news that Sam was back in the country.

He was working in the city. He was a

玛利亚不能再等下去了。

她要去和他一起住在城市里。当然，他会在城市找到一份好工作。

一天，周太太来告诉她。有人说，山姆回国了。

他在城市工作，是一个年轻的律师。玛利亚很激动。

young lawyer. Maria's heart was beating   beat *v.* 跳动

fast with joy.

Mrs Choo said, "I don't know why he did not come and see you. I don't know why he did not tell you."

Maria said, "Oh, he must be busy. I will go and see him in the city."

She was thinking. Sam was too busy to come back to visit her. She would visit him in the city.

周太太说："我不知道他为什么不来看你。我不知道他为什么不告诉你。"

玛利亚说："哦，他一定很忙。我要去城市看他。"

她在想：山姆太忙了，不能回来看她，她要去城市找他。

That night, she asked Kate to go and get Sam's office address from Mrs Choo. She would go the next morning. She could not wait to see him.

address *n.* 地址

Kate was worried about her aunt going to the city alone.

worried *adj.* 担心的

"Aunt Maria, let me go with you."

But, her aunt said, "No need. You must go to school. I'll take the bus. I will be all right."

那天晚上，她让凯特去向周太太要山姆的办公室地址。明天一早，她就要去看山姆。她急着去见他。

凯特不放心姨妈一个人去城市。

"玛利亚姨妈，让我陪你去吧。"

但是，她的姨妈说："没有必要。你得去上学。我坐公共汽车去，不会有事的。"

She was so sure Sam would be happy to see her. Of course, he would be happy to see his mother.

Early the next morning, Maria took the first bus to the city.

The bus journey was two hours. It seemed like two years to her.

journey *n.* 旅程

By noon, she was at the bus station in the city.

She then took a taxi to Sam's office.

他相信山姆见到她一定会很开心。见到妈妈，他当然会很开心。

第二天一早，玛利亚坐上了去城市的第一班汽车。

路上的两个小时像两年那么长。

中午的时候，她到了城市的长途汽车站。

然后她乘出租车去山姆的办公室。她把地址告诉给司机。出租

She showed the address to the taxi driver. The taxi stopped in front of a tall building.

Maria entered the building. The security guard asked her who she was looking for.

security *n.* 安全

She told him Sam's name. She showed him the name of his office. He went with her into the lift. They went up to the tenth

lift *n.* 电梯

车停在一幢高楼前面。

玛利亚走进大楼。保安问她找谁。

她说了山姆的名字和山姆的办公室。保安陪着她进了电梯。他们一直上到十楼。

floor.

She got out of the lift. The guard
pointed the door to her.

point *v.* 指

Maria expected her son to welcome
her. He would hug her with tears. But,
Sam did not. He saw an old lady in an
old pantsuit.

expect *v.* 期待

pantsuit *n.*

She looked tired. And she was asking
for him.

（女子的）衣裤套装

His staff all looked at him. They were

staff *n.* 同事

她走出电梯。保安给她指了路。

玛利亚期待着儿子会欢迎她，会眼含热泪地拥抱她。但是，山姆并没有。他看见了这个穿着破旧工作服的老太太。

她看起来很累。她说找山姆。

同事们都看着他。他们想："这个女人是谁？为什么要找山

wondering, "Who is this woman? Why is she asking for Sam?"

wonder v. 好奇

Sam pretended he did not know her. He asked the security guard to chase her out.

pretend v. 假装

chase v. 追；赶

He said, "I don't know this woman! She must not be in the office."

Poor Maria was shocked. She pushed away the security guard's hand and ran out of the office. She cried all the way

shocked adj. 震惊的

姆？"

山姆假装不认识她。他让保安把她赶出去。

他说："我不认识这个女人！她不能待在办公室。"

可怜的玛利亚惊呆了。她推开保安的手，冲出了办公室，一路

名人名言

Think twice before you do.

三思而后行。

home.

Her heart was breaking into pieces.

Kate was waiting for her aunt. She saw Maria's tears. She knew everything.

A week passed. Maria was not the same person.

She could not eat. She could not sleep. She was talking to herself.

She looked at Sam's old photographs and cried all the time. "Where is my son?

break *v.* 破碎

哭着回家了。

她的心碎了。

凯特正在等姨妈。看到玛利亚眼中的泪水，她明白了一切。

一个星期过去了。玛利亚完全变了一个人。

她吃不下，睡不着，总是自言自语。

她看着山姆的照片，一直在哭："我的儿子在哪儿？回到我身

Come back to me, my son."

It was one afternoon. Maria was looking at the album crying.

album *n.* 影集

Something made her look up. Someone was standing at the door.

It was Sam! Sam realized he was in the wrong. His mother came to look for him. He chased her out of his office.

realize *v.* 认识到

A few days ago, Kate phoned him to tell him he was wrong to do that. Kate

边吧，儿子。"

一天下午，玛利亚正在看着影集哭。

她抬起头。有人站在门口。

是山姆！山姆知道他错了。妈妈来找他，他却把她赶出了办公室。

几天前，凯特给他打电话，告诉他这样做是不对的。凯特告诉

told him about his mother's love for him.

It was Sunday. After the phone call, Sam took the bus and came home to see his mother.

He came home to ask her to forgive him. He was not a good son.

forgive v. 原谅

Maria stopped crying.

She jumped up and said, "My son is back! My son is here!"

She was so happy.

他，他的母亲很爱他。

今天是星期日。接到电话后，山姆坐车回家看望母亲。

他回家请求她的原谅。他不是个好儿子。

玛利亚不哭了。

她跳起来说："我的儿子回来了！我的儿子在这里！"

她是如此的开心。

Sacrifice of Love

爱的牺牲

Lay Hoon and her brother, John, are orphans. John is younger than her by a year.

orphan *n.* 孤儿

Their parents died in a car accident two years ago. They died on the spot. It was a tragic day.

tragic *adj.* 悲惨的

Their parents went to visit their grandmother. On the way home, it was raining heavily. Their car hit a tree. The car smashed into pieces.

smash *v.* 撞碎

丽云和弟弟约翰是孤儿。约翰比她小一岁。

他们的父母在两年前的车祸中去世了。他们当场死亡，那是场悲剧。

父母去拜访祖母。在回家的路上，下着大雨，他们的车撞在了树上，撞成了碎片。

It took Lay Hoon and John a long time to get over the death of their parents. They were very close to their parents.

get over
从……中恢复常态

Now, they have only each other.

They care deeply for each other. If Lay Hoon is sick or sad, John can feel it too. It is the same with Lay Hoon. She can feel what John feels.

They try to make each other happy. Lay Hoon cooks the meals.

丽云和约翰用了很长一段时间才从失去父母的悲痛中解脱出来。他们跟父母的感情很深。

现在，他们相依为命。

他们非常关心对方。如果丽云生病或者不开心，约翰也同她一起不开心。丽云也会跟约翰一样感同身受。

他们努力让对方快乐。丽云负责做饭。

John is stronger. So, he does the heavy household chores.

Lay Hoon loves cooking and baking. She loves to prepare meals for John.

As for John, he loves to ride on a motorbike. He owns an old motorbike. He bought a second-hand bike a year ago. And he takes good care of it.

One day, they were walking along the street. They passed some shops.

chore *n.* 日常事务

bake *v.* 烘焙

prepare *v.* 准备

motorbike *n.* 摩托车

约翰更强壮一些。因此，家里的那些重活儿都由他负责。

丽云喜欢烹饪和烘焙。她喜欢为约翰做饭。

至于约翰，他喜欢骑摩托车。他有一辆旧摩托车。一年前，他买了这辆二手车。他很爱护这辆车。

有一天，他们走在街上，经过一些商店。

It was the month of May. Their birthdays would be next week. Both have their birthdays in May. Lay Hoon's birthday is one day earlier. So, they celebrate their birthdays at the same time. And every year, they buy presents for each other.

Lay Hoon asked John, "What can I get for you this year? Your birthday is next

celebrate *v.* 庆祝

at the same time 同时

已经是五月份了。他们的生日在下周。他们俩的生日都在五月。丽云的生日比约翰早一天。所以,他们总是同时庆祝生日。每年,他们都会为对方买生日礼物。

丽云问约翰:"今年我能送你点什么?下周就是你的生日了,

week. What would you like?"

John asked her the same question, "What can I get for you this year? Your birthday is next week. What do you want?"

They are happy buying presents for each other. On the same day, they give each other presents.

When their parents were alive, the whole family celebrated the birthdays of

你想要点什么？"

约翰也问了同样的问题："我能给你买点什么呢？你的生日是下个星期。你想要什么？"

他们很高兴能够为彼此购买礼物。在同一天，把礼物送给对方。

父母还健在的时候，全家人一起为丽云和约翰庆祝生日，那是

Lay Hoon and John. It was a very happy occasion.

occasion *n.* 场合

Their father and mother knew exactly what Lay and John wanted.

exactly *adv.* 准确地

Lay Hoon usually got accessories like jade ear-rings or a set of silver chain and bracelet.

accessory *n.* 配饰

bracelet *n.* 手镯

John would get a set of garden tools for his favourite pastime, gardening.

非常快乐的场合。

他们的父母总是知道，丽云和约翰想要什么。

丽云通常会收到一件首饰，比如一对儿玉耳环，一条银项链或者银手镯。

约翰会得到一整套园林工具。因为他最喜欢的消遣是园艺。

Lay Hoon and John came to a street with all types of shops. There is a shop selling motorbikes and accessories.

The accessories are the motorbike light, seat, mirror and carrier at the back.

carrier *n.* 货架

The shop also sells motorbike riders' suits. This is for motorbike riders to wear when riding their motorbikes.

suit *n.* 服装

A complete motorbike rider's suit has

complete *adj.* 完整的

丽云和约翰来到商店林立的街道。那里有一家销售摩托车及配件的商店。

这些配件包括摩托车灯，座椅，镜子以及车后的货架。

这家商店也卖摩托车服。就是摩托车手骑摩托时穿的衣服。

一套完整的摩托车服包括安全头盔、皮上衣、皮裤子、皮手套

a safety helmet, a leather jacket, leather pants, leather gloves and leather boots. It looks smart. And it is quite expensive.

The motorbike rider looks smart in it. Many motorbike riders would love to own this suit. It is the suitable outfit to wear when riding a motorbike.

The whole suit protects the motorbike rider. The helmet protects his head. The jacket and pants protect his body. The

helmet *n.* 头盔

boot *n.* 靴子

suitable *adj.* 合适的

outfit *n.* 全套服装

和皮靴。它看上去很漂亮。价钱也相当昂贵。

摩托车服穿起来很帅气。很多摩托车手都想要一套这样的衣服。它很适合在骑摩托车时穿。

它能全面保护摩托车手。头盔保护头部，皮衣和裤子保护身

gloves protect his hands. The leather shoes protect his feet.

protect *v.* 保护

It keeps out the hot sun. It also protects the motorbike rider from the dust and strong wind.

John passed the shop. He stopped at the entrance.

entrance *n.* 入口

That was not the first time he saw the suit. He saw it many times. He would never get tired of looking at it.

体，手套保护手，皮鞋保护脚。

　　它阻隔了炎热的阳光，保护摩托车手不受灰尘和强风的侵袭。

　　约翰走过商店，停在门口。

　　这不是他第一次看这套衣服了。他看过了很多次了，百看不厌。

名人名言

Things at the worst will mend.

否极泰来。

He stared at the motorbike rider's suit through the glass door. Of course, he would like to own one like that. But, he could not tell Lay Hoon.

own *v.* 拥有

John was thinking, "I can't say I want this for my birthday. It costs $600. It's just too expensive."

expensive *adj.*

昂贵的

"I would buy if I have money. But, where can I get so much money?"

He passed the shop and sighed.

sigh *v.* 叹气

他透过玻璃门，盯着摩托车服看。当然，他想拥有一套这样的车服。但是，他不能告诉丽云。

约翰心里想："我不能说我想要这套车服做生日礼物。它要600美元，太贵了。"

"等我有了钱，我就买。但是，我能到哪里赚这么多钱呢？"

他走过商店，叹了口气。

Lay Hoon knew what he was thinking. She knew he wanted the jacket very much. But, he would not tell her.

Then, they passed a jewellery shop.

jewellery *n.* 珠宝

This time, Lay Hoon stared at the shop. Through the glass door, she saw a gold bracelet. She saw it many times. It looked so classy. It would look nice on a girl's wrist.

classy *adj.* 上等的

wrist *n.* 手腕

She would love to wear it on her wrist.

丽云知道他在想什么。她知道他非常想要那件衣服。但是，他不会告诉她。

然后，他们来到了一家珠宝店。

这一次，轮到丽云盯着商店看了。透过玻璃门，她看见一只金手镯。她看过很多次了。它看起来是那么的优雅，戴在女孩子的手腕上一定很漂亮。

她很想把它戴在手腕上，可800美元，她没有那么多钱。

It cost $800. She did not have so much money.

She was thinking too, "I can't tell John this is what I want. It's just too expensive."

John knew what she was thinking. He knew his sister would love the bracelet as a birthday present.

bracelet *n.* 手镯

So, they passed the shops and walked slowly home. They did not buy any

～～～～～～～～～～～～～～～～～～

她也在想："我不能让约翰知道我想要这只手镯，它太贵了。"

约翰知道她在想什么。他知道他的姐姐想要这只手镯作为生日礼物。

就这样，他们走过了很多家商店，慢慢地走回家。他们没买任

presents.

They would buy the presents another day.

Back home, Lay Hoon cooked John's favourite meal. This was seafood pasta.

pasta *n.* 意大利面

John liked his pasta spicy. So, Lay Hoon added chilli sauce. She liked to prepare her own chilli sauce.

chilli *n.* 辣椒

sauce *n.* 酱

On the shelf were six bottles of different sauce flavours. She knew John

何礼物。

他们想改天再去买。

回到家里，丽云做了约翰最喜欢的菜——海鲜意大利面。

约翰喜欢吃辣味意大利面。所以，丽云放了辣椒酱。她喜欢自己做辣椒酱。

架子上有六瓶不同风味的酱料。她知道约翰喜欢在吃鱼、肉或

liked to eat his fish or meat or noodles with chilli sauce. Nothing pleased her more than preparing food for John.

That night, Lay Hoon counted her savings. She had just $200.

But, she needed $600. So, she needed $400.

How was she to get $400? That night, she could not sleep. She was thinking of how to get $400 to buy the motorbike

please *v.*
使……开心

count *v.* 数

saving *n.* 积蓄

面条时放辣椒酱。没有什么比为约翰准备食物更令她高兴的了。

那天晚上，丽云数了一下她的积蓄。她只有200美元。

可那件车服要600美元。所以，她还需要400美元。

她怎么能得到400美元呢？那天晚上，她睡不着。她在想怎么

rider's suit for John. She must buy it. It would make her brother so happy.

The next morning, she got up early. She knew what to do.

She looked at the mirror in her room. She stood in front of the mirror. She stared at her reflection in the mirror. It showed a pretty girl with long hair.

reflection *n.* 映像

Then, she looked at her long, lovely shiny black hair.

shiny *adj.* 有光泽的

能得到400美元为约翰买车服。她要买下它。这会使弟弟开心的。

第二天早上,她很早就起床了。她知道要怎么做。

她看着房间的镜子。她站到了镜子前面,盯着镜子中的自己。她看到一个漂亮的女孩,留着一头长发。

然后,她看着自己那头长长的乌黑亮丽的秀发。

It reached to below her knees. She always let it hang freely.

knee *n.* 膝盖

hang *v.* 悬挂

It fell around her like a beautiful cloak. Her friends said it made her look like a princess.

cloak *n.* 斗篷

The hair would bring some money.

She touched her hair lovingly. She was always proud of her long lovely hair.

lovingly *adv.* 深情地

Lay Hoon started keeping her hair long at the age of four. At that age, she was

它长及膝盖。她总是散披着头发。

头发披在她身上就像一件漂亮的斗篷。朋友们说，这使她看起来像一个公主。

头发会给她换来一些钱。

她深情地触摸着自己的秀发。这头长长的秀发总是令她很自豪。

丽云四岁就开始留头发。那时，她个子很矮，比很多同年龄的

small in size. She was smaller than other girls of that age.

Her mother let her hair grow.

Her mother used to say, "You are my little princess in the tower. You let your hair down. It can become a ladder for you to climb down from the tower."

ladder *n.* 梯子

Lay Hoon loved that fairy tale. She made her mother tell her the story again and again.

fairy tale 童话故事

女孩要矮。

母亲让她留头发。

母亲说，"你是我的塔楼里的小公主。你把头发放下来，它就可以变成梯子，你就可以从塔楼里爬下来了。"

丽云喜欢这个童话故事。她让母亲给她讲了很多遍。

She often heard comments about her hair. "What lovely hair!"

Her mother used to tell her, "Your hair can make good shampoo advertisements."

Her friends also said, "I wish I had hair like yours."

Yes, she had lovely hair indeed. And she could sell her lovely hair to get some money.

comment *n.* 评论

shampoo *n.* 洗发水

advertisement *n.* 广告

她经常听到别人赞赏她的头发："多么漂亮的头发呀！"

母亲曾经对她说："你可以去拍洗发水广告了。"

朋友们也说："真希望我也能拥有像你一样的秀发。"

是的，她确实有头漂亮的头发。她可以卖掉头发换钱。

  名人名言

Time and tide wait for no man.

时不我待。

She was so proud of her lovely hair.
She knew selling her hair would hurt her
mother. Her mother would be saying,
"My baby girl's hair is gone."

But, she also knew her mother would
understand why she did it.

understand *v.* 理解

Losing her hair to buy a birthday
present for her brother was a good
reason.

reason *n.* 理由

Her hair could grow again. John could

她为她的秀发感到骄傲。她知道卖掉头发会伤害母亲。母亲会说："我宝贝女儿的长头发没了。"

但是，她也知道她母亲能够理解她为什么这样做。

卖掉头发，给弟弟买生日礼物，就是个很好的理由。

头发可以再长出来。而约翰在生日那一天能得到喜欢的生日礼

get the birthday present he liked that day.

She pinned up her hair slowly. She stood still in front of the mirror.

pin *v.* 固定

A tear dropped from her eyes and onto the floor. She refused to think any further. Her mind was made up.

refuse *v.* 拒绝

Quickly, she put on her old brown coat.

Then, she ran out of the door and down the stairs to the street.

物。

她慢慢地盘起头发。在镜子前站了一会儿。

一滴眼泪从她的眼中落在了地板上。她不想再想了。她主意已定。

她迅速穿上棕色的旧外套。

然后，她走下楼，来到了街上。

In the hair salon, she sold her hair. The hairdresser cut her long lovely hair.

She first asked Lay Hoon, "Are you sure?"

She nodded. She managed to get $400 for her lovely hair.

She left the shop thinking, "It's worth it. John will love his birthday present this year."

She hurried to the motorbike shop.

salon	*n.* 美发厅
hairdresser	*n.* 理发师
manage	*v.* 勉力完成
hurry	*v.* 匆忙

在理发店，她卖掉了头发，理发师为她剪头发。

她先问丽云："你确定吗？"

她点头。她想方设法把头发卖了400美元。

她离开理发店的时候想："这是值得的。约翰会喜欢他今年的生日礼物的。"

她急忙来到摩托车店。

An hour later, she came home. She was holding John's birthday present. It was in a plastic bag.

plastic *n.* 塑料

John was sitting on the stool waiting for her. He was worried about where she went to.

stool *n.* 凳子

When he saw her with her new haircut, he simply stared at her.

haircut *n.* 发型

He asked, "Sis, what have you done to your lovely hair?"

一小时后，她回到家，手里拿着约翰的生日礼物。它装在一个塑料袋里。

约翰正坐在凳子上等她。他正在担心她去了哪里。

当他看到梳着新发型的她，他只是盯着她看。

他问，"姐姐，你的头发哪儿去了？"

Lay Hoon put on a smiling face. She just said, "Oh, I decided to cut it."

decide v. 决定

John continued, "But, you love your hair. You kept it for years. Why did you cut it?"

continue v. 继续

She smiled at him holding the plastic bag.

Lay Hoon said, "Don't talk about my hair. I bought you your birthday present."

Happily, she took out the motorbike

丽云摆出一张笑脸。她说："哦，我把它剪了。"

约翰接着说："但是，你喜欢你的头发。你留了很多年，为什么剪掉它？"

她拿着塑料袋向他微笑。

丽云说："不要说我的头发了。我为你买了生日礼物。"

她高兴地从塑料袋里拿出了摩托车服。

rider's suit from the plastic bag.

It was pure leather. The jacket, the pants, the gloves and the boots!

pure *adj.* 纯的

leather *n.* 皮革

That was Just what John wanted! He wondered how she got the money to buy it.

wonder *v.* 好奇

John knew. He said softly, "You cut your hair and sold it to get the money to buy me a birthday present."

Lay Hoon said, "Look, I've got your

它是纯皮的。夹克，裤子，手套和靴子！

正是约翰想要的！他正在琢磨她从哪儿来的钱。

约翰猜到了。他轻轻地说，"你把头发剪了，用卖头发的钱给我买了生日礼物。"

丽云说："看，我给你买了摩托车服。不要再想我的头发了。

motorbike rider's suit. Never mind about my hair. It will grow again. What's more important is you like your present."

mind *v.* 关心

And she asked him, "Do you like it?"

John could only hug her tightly. He nodded his head. He could not say a word.

tightly *adv.* 紧紧地

nod *v.* 点头

There was no need . He understood the sacrifice she made for him.

sacrifice *n.* 牺牲

She sold her hair to get him a birthday

它还会再长出来的。重要的是，你喜欢你的礼物。"

她问他："你喜欢吗？"

约翰只是紧紧地拥抱着她。他点着头，一句话儿也说不出来。

不需要这样做的。他清楚她为自己做出了牺牲。

她卖掉头发为了买他喜欢的生日礼物，这是她送的最好的礼

present he liked. It was the best present she could give. Her birthday present to him was a sacrifice of love.

John then told her he sold his motorbike. He sold it to get the money to buy her a birthday present.

And, he took it out from a box. It was the gold bracelet!

She stared at it. She cried tears of joy.

He wanted to make her happy with a

tear *n.* 泪水

物。她送给他的生日礼物就是为爱做出的牺牲。

约翰告诉她他卖掉了摩托车，这样他就可以给她买生日礼物了。

然后，他从盒子里拿出礼物。是那只金手镯！

她看着手镯。眼睛里流着喜悦的泪水。

他想送她喜爱的生日礼物使她快乐。他送出的生日礼物也是为

birthday present she liked. His birthday present to her was also a sacrifice of love.

Lay Hoon said, "What! Why did you do that? Now you have a motorbike rider's suit without a motorbike."

And he said the same thing, "Look, I've got your gold bracelet. Never mind about my motorbike. I will save money. So, I can buy one again."

save *v.* 储蓄；攒钱

爱做出的牺牲。

丽云说："什么！为什么做那样的事呢？现在你拥有了摩托车服却没有了摩托车。"

他也说了同样的话："看，我为你买了金手镯。不要管我的摩托车。我会存钱。这样，我就可以再买一辆了。"

She hugged him back. There was no need for her to say anything.

hug *v.* 拥抱

And so sister and brother gave their presents to each other.

It was the best present they could have. The present was bought by selling something they both liked.

Yes, it was their sacrifice of love for each other. And the sacrifice was made with a lot of joy. The sacrifice was the birthday present.

~~~~~~

她也拥抱了弟弟。她不需要说话。

于是，姐弟俩都给了对方礼物。

是他们能买得起的最好的礼物。他们卖掉了喜欢的东西，给对方买了礼物。

是的，这是他们为对方做出的爱的牺牲。心甘情愿地为对方做出牺牲。这种牺牲本身就是生日礼物。

MCGRAW-HILL

The Poor Fishman

可怜的渔夫

Hassan was a fisherman. He lived in a quiet and peaceful fishing village.

His village was near the sea. His father was a fisherman too. So was his grandfather.

Fishing was their first love. To them, it was a good job. His sons would also be fishermen. He would pass his boats to them.

Hassan lived with his wife and three

peaceful *adj.* 平和的

fisherman *n.* 渔夫

哈桑是个渔夫。他住在一个宁静平和的渔村里。

他的村庄就在海边。他的父亲也是渔夫。祖父也是渔夫。

捕鱼是他们的最爱。对他们来说，这是一个很好的工作。他的儿子将来也会成为渔夫。他会把船传给他们。

哈桑与妻子和三个儿子生活在一起。他们虽然贫穷但很快乐。

sons. They were poor but happy.

He was a good father. His wife was a good mother. She cooked all their meals. Of course, she cooked fish every day.

Her sons liked fried fish. They also liked fish curry and chilli fish. She made good fish curry.

His three sons were still too young to help him fish. They were going to the only village school nearby.

fry *v.* 油炸

curry *n.* 咖喱菜

他是个好父亲。妻子也是个好母亲。她为他们做饭。当然，她每天都会做鱼。

儿子们喜欢吃炸鱼。他们还喜欢咖喱鱼和辣酱鱼。她的咖喱鱼做得很好。

儿子们还太小，不能帮他捕鱼。他们在家附近的村里唯一的学校读书。

But, they could row the boat very well like their father. Like their father, they loved fishing.

row *v.* 划（船）

They loved the sea. This was the only place they knew. And they did not want to leave their village.

Hassan woke up early every morning. It was as early as six o'clock. He had a heavy breakfast with his wife.

wake *v.* 醒；醒来

After breakfast, he got ready his fishing

但是，他们像父亲一样，船划得很好。跟父亲一样，他们喜欢捕鱼。

他们爱大海。这儿是唯一一个他们熟悉的地方，他们不想离开自己的村庄。

哈桑每天起得很早。早上六点钟就起来了。他与妻子一起享用一顿丰盛的早餐。

早饭后，他准备好渔网和鱼线。

net and line.

Then, he put on his big straw hat. He walked to the shore. It was ten minutes' walk from his house. He always enjoyed the morning walk.

That morning, he woke up very early. It was still dark.

His wife was in the kitchen preparing breakfast. She was frying his favourite fried rice.

net *n.* 网

straw *n.* 稻草

enjoy *v.* 享受

prepare *v.* 准备

然后，戴上他的大草帽，走到海边。海边离他家步行只需要十分钟。他总是很享受这段路程。

那天早上，他很早就醒了，天还是黑的。

他的妻子正在厨房准备早餐。她做得是他最喜欢的炒饭。

She asked him, "It's only four o'clock. Why are you up so early?" She told him to go back to bed.

Hassan told her, "I can't sleep any more. I have this feeling something will happen today. Today's fishing is going to be different."

happen v. 发生
different adj. 不同的

She looked at him, "I hope it is not bad weather."

weather n. 天气

The weather can be stormy on some

stormy adj. 暴风雨的

她问他："现在才四点。你为什么起得这么早？"她让他回床上再睡会儿。

哈桑告诉她："我睡不着。我有种感觉，今天会发生点什么。捕鱼时会有不同的经历。"

她看着他说道："我希望不会遇到坏天气。"

有时会有暴风雨发生。

days.

Hassan looked at her.

Fishermen had to be careful of bad weather. They should turn back.

During thunderstorm, boats would be overturned and sank.

Many fishermen drowned. They did not come back alive.

Hassan then answered, "No, the weather is fine. I think it is something

careful *adj.* 小心的

thunderstorm *n.* 暴风雨

overturn *v.* 翻掉; 倾倒

drown *v.* 淹死; 溺死

哈桑看着她。

渔民必须小心坏天气。他们必须安全地回到岸上。

暴风雨发生时，船会被打翻，沉到海里。

许多渔夫在暴风雨中淹死了，他们没能活着回来。

哈桑回答说："不，今天天气很好。我觉得会有好事发生。"

good for us."

Hassan and his wife sat down to a very early breakfast. They ate the fried rice. He ate it with curry fish.

Sometimes, she packed him lunch in a big box. He could eat his meal at sea.

pack *v.* 装（箱）

He was still thinking, "Today something is going to happen. I know it. Something tells me that."

After breakfast, Hassan walked to the

哈桑和妻子早早地就吃了早餐。他们吃的是炒饭和咖喱鱼。

有时，她会给他带一大盒午餐让他在海上吃。

他还是觉得："今天会发生点什么事儿。我知道，我有预感。"

吃完早饭，哈桑走到海边。太早了，岸上一个人也没有。

shore. It was early. There was nobody on the shore yet.

He looked at the sky. The weather was fine. It was not going to rain. There would be no lightning or thunder.

Fishermen were good at telling the weather. They had to know the weather.

Hassan had a partner. They always fished together. They owned the boat.

Both of them bought a good

lightning *n.* 闪电

thunder *n.* 雷

partner *n.* 同伴

own *v.* 拥有

他抬头看看天空。天气晴朗，不会下雨，也不会有雷电。

渔民们擅长预测天气。他们必须了解天气。

哈桑有一个伙伴。他们总是在一起捕鱼。他们共同拥有那艘船。

他们一起买了一艘很不错的摩托艇，艇上装有性能优良的引

motorboat. The boat had a good engine. A motorboat was better than a sampan.

A motorboat did not need paddling. They put on the engine and it moved in the water. It could move fast. It could take them far out to the sea.

So, Hassan and his partner were happy with their motorboat. Some day, they had a good catch. They would bring home fifteen to twenty medium-sized

motorboat *n.* 摩托艇

sampan *n.* 舢板

paddle *v.* 用桨划船

擎。摩托艇要比舢板船好得多。

摩托艇不需要桨。安上发动机，它们就能在水中行进了。它可以开得很快，可以开到远海。

因此，哈桑和他的伙伴对他们的摩托艇很满意。有时，他们运

名人名言

Time flies.

光阴似箭。

fish weighing between 350 gram and 500 gram.

gram *n.* 克

They sold the fish to the fish dealer. They brought home the smaller ones for their wives to fry for dinner. And they had some money to buy rice and vegetables.

dealer *n.* 交易商

His partner was not on the shore yet. So, Hassan took a walk on the beach. He looked at the calm sea.

calm *adj.* 平静的

He was thinking, "I love the sea. I was

气好。他们会带回十五到二十条350克到500克中等大小的鱼。

他们把这些鱼卖给鱼贩子，小一点的带回家给妻子做晚餐。这样，他们就有钱买大米和蔬菜了。

他的伙伴还没来。因此，哈桑在海滩上散步。他看着平静的海面。

他想："我爱大海。我在这里出生，也要死在这里。我不会去

born here near the sea. I will die here. I will not go anywhere else."

And he was thinking too. So would his sons and their sons.

A while later, his partner came. His name was Ah Chong.

Ah Chong saw Hassan and shouted, "You are early this morning. Why? Are you expecting a big catch?" Every fisherman hoped for a big catch every

shout v. 喊叫

expect v. 期待

catch n. 总捕获量

别的地方。"

他也想着他的子孙后代也会跟自己一样。

过了一会儿，他的伙伴来了。他叫阿忠。

阿忠看到哈桑喊道，"你今天很早啊。为什么呢？期待捕到大

day.

And Hassan, "We'll see, we'll see. Our luck will come."

The two men untied the rope to their | untie v. 解开
boat. They pushed it into the water.

Then, they got on board the boat. It was not a big boat. But, it was a good strong one.

They were quite happy with it. Hassan told Ah Chong, "One day, we catch more

鱼吗？"渔夫们每天都期待捕到大鱼。

哈桑说："等着瞧。我们的运气来了。"

他们俩解开缆绳，把船推下水。

然后，他们上了船。船不大，但很结实。

他们对它很满意。哈桑告诉阿忠："等我们捕到更多的鱼，我

fish. We will buy a bigger boat."

They were far out in the sea now. Soon, they settled down at a suitable spot. Hassan cast his fishing line.

There were a few pulls. He reeled it in each time. But, there was nothing at the end of the line.

Sometimes, they had to wait for an hour or two. Ah Chong cast his line and waited too.

suitable *adj.* 合适的

cast *v.* 投；抛

们就买一条更大的船。"

这时他们来到了远海。很快，他们把船停在了合适的地方。哈桑投下了鱼线。

鱼线被拉动过几次。每次他都收线。但底下什么都没有。

有时，他们要等一两个小时。阿忠也把渔线投入水中，等鱼上钩。

After nine o'clock, the sun was getting hot. There was still no catch. The sun was beating down hard on them.

Both fishermen were thinking, "Today, the fish are clever. They are not eating the worms."

worm *n.* 幼虫

It looked like it was going to be a long day. The two men started to sigh. There were many such days.

sigh *v.* 叹息

On bad days, they would be lucky to

　　九点以后，太阳越来越热了。还是没有什么收获。太阳直射在他们身上。

　　他们想："今天，鱼很聪明，他们不吃鱼饵。"

　　看起来今天会在海上呆很长时间了。他们俩开始叹息。有过许多这样的日子。

　　运气不好的时候，能捕到五条中等大小的鱼就很不错了。

catch five medium-sized fish.

Hassan was thinking, "Is this the feeling I had the whole morning? Is it another bad day?"

He was feeling sad. Maybe, he was hoping for too much. But, he was so sure today would be different.

Then, he felt a slight tug. Hassan began to reel in his fishing line. It could be just a small fish.

medium-sized *adj.*
中等大小的

tug *n* （突然的）猛拉；
猛拽

　　哈桑想："难道这就是我整个早上的预感？会是另一个糟糕的一天吗？"

　　他感到悲伤。也许他期望的太高了。但他肯定今天会有所不同。

　　然后，他感到鱼线被轻轻拖动了一下，哈桑开始收线。有可能只是一条小鱼。

He was thinking, "Well, at least something." They were in the sea for three hours already.

Ah Chong looked at him pulling in the fishing line.

Hassan wound the fishing line. The tugs on the fishing line became stronger.

wind v. 转动

It was going to be a big fish. He was feeling happier.

Soon, he was struggling with the fish.

struggle v. 斗争；
抗争

他想，"嗯，至少有收获。"他们已经在海上钓了三个小时了。

阿忠看到他在收线。

哈桑摇着鱼线。鱼线下的拖动变强了。

这会是一条大鱼，他变得高兴起来。

很快，他就跟鱼较量起来。

Ah Chong had to help him. He put aside his own line. Together with Hassan, he pulled harder and harder.

Both men were pulling and reeling the line. They did it again and again. It took them a full hour to do this.

Hassan was shouting, "It has to be a big box."

Ah Chong agreed with him. Yes, it had to be a big box. No fish was that heavy.

put aside 放置一边

agree *v.* 同意

阿忠不得不去帮他。他把自己的鱼线放在一边。与哈桑一起，使劲儿拉。

他们俩一边拉线一边绕线。绕了一圈又一圈。他们整整花了一个小时。

哈桑喊叫着："肯定是个大箱子。"

阿忠也同意他的想法。是的，一定是个大箱子。没有鱼会这么重。

MCGRAW-HILL

On some days, they pulled up a box.
Or they pulled up a big bag.

People threw all kinds of things in the
sea. There was one time they pulled up a
big plastic bag of rubbish.

Hassan said, "I don't know how people
can do this. They throw rubbish in the   rubbish *n.* 垃圾
sea. The water gets dirty. Their children
swim in the sea and get skin problem."   problem *n.* 麻烦

Hassan and Ah Chong pulled in the

有时候，他们会钓到盒子或袋子。

人们把各种各样的东西扔到海里。有一次，他们钓到一塑料袋
垃圾。

哈桑说："我不知道人们怎么能这么做。他们把垃圾扔进大
海，弄脏了海水。他们的孩子在海里游泳，就会得皮肤病。"

哈桑和阿忠拉到最后的几米鱼线。他们真正感觉到了分量。它

last few metres of the fishing line. They
really felt the weight. It was very heavy.

weight *n.* 重量

    They were thinking, "Maybe, twenty
kilograms or more. Oh good!" That would
be their day.

kilogram *n.* 公斤；
               千克

    They were hoping it was a big fish.
That would be enough catch for one day.
That would bring them some money after
selling the fish.

    They did not want to hope for more.

很重。

    他们想："也许，超过二十公斤。噢，真好！"这是他们的好
日子。

    他们希望这是一条大鱼，今天的收获就足够了。卖了鱼，他们
可以剩一些钱。

    他们没有更高的奢望。

But, they were in for a pleasant surface. Their catch was an ikan toman. And it weighed a heavy 62 kilograms! Both men shouted out loudly. They jumped up and down in their boat.

pleasant *adj.* 可喜的

They just could not believe their eyes.

The other fishermen could hear them. They knew it must be a big catch. But, nobody expected an ikan toman.

They all went near Hassan's boat.

但是，他们得到了一个大大的惊喜。他们捕到了一条托曼鱼。它重达62公斤！两人高声喊叫。他们在船上高兴地直跳。

他们不敢相信自己的眼睛。

其他渔民听到了他们的喊声。他们知道，一定是捕到了大鱼。但是，没有人想到会是一条托曼鱼。

他们都来到哈桑的船边。事实上，这是他们见过的最大的托曼

Indeed, it was the biggest ikan toman they ever saw.

It was on board the boat now. It was as heavy as a man!

Hassan and Ah Chong quickly rowed their boat to the shore.

The two fishermen carried the huge | huge *adj.* 巨大的
fish to the beach. By now, everyone from the village heard about their catch.

They were shouting at each other.

鱼。

它就在船的甲板上。有一个人那么重！

哈桑和阿忠很快把船划到了岸边。

他们把这条巨大的鱼抬到了海滩上。现在，村里的每个人都听说了这件事。

他们互相喊着："哈桑捕到了最大的托曼鱼。来亲眼看看

 名人名言

Time is money.

时间就是金钱。

"Hassan caught the biggest ikan toman. Come and see for yourself."

And everyone from the old man to the child came running to look at the fish. It was indeed the biggest fish they ever saw.

News about Hassan's catch spread very quickly. Soon people from other villages came to his village to see for themselves. They went back and talked

spread v. 传播

吧。"

从老人到孩子，每个人都跑过来看这条鱼。这确实是他们见过的最大的鱼。

关于哈桑捕到大鱼的消息传得很快。不久，其他村庄的人也都来他们村亲眼看鱼。他们回去后，跟其他人谈论着这条鱼。

about the fish to other people.

It was the catch of the year!

They all said the same thing, "It must be the biggest ikan toman in the sea. Lucky Hassan and Ah Chong for catching it."

According to the Fishery Department, that catch was the biggest ever.

| department *n.* 部门

News reporters came and took pictures of the fish. The picture of Hassan and

| reporter *n.* 记者

它是一年中捕到的最大的鱼！

他们都说："那一定是海里最大的托曼鱼。幸运的哈桑和阿忠捕到了它。"

根据渔业部的记载，那是有史以来捕到的最大的鱼。

新闻记者来为这条鱼拍照。哈桑和阿忠上了报纸的头版。

Ah Chong was on the front page of the newspaper.

Offers to buy the fish began to pour in.

pour *v.* 不断涌现

Hassan's life changed after this. From a poor fisherman, he was now a famous person.

But, he did not want to change his life. He continued fishing. He and Ah Chong bought a bigger boat.

~~~~~~

来买鱼的人络绎不绝。之后，哈桑的生活变了。从一个贫穷的渔夫，变成了现在的名人。

但是，他不想改变自己的生活。他继续捕鱼。他和阿忠买了一条更大的船。